Dividing Rivers

poems by

Ivy Schweitzer

Finishing Line Press
Georgetown, Kentucky

Dividing Rivers

*For do-overs,
and for Grace Paley, who also began again*

Copyright © 2025 by Ivy Schweitzer
ISBN 979-8-89990-072-3 First Edition
All rights reserved under International and Pan-American Copyright Conventions. No part of this book may be reproduced in any manner whatsoever without written permission from the publisher, except in the case of brief quotations embodied in critical articles and reviews.

Publisher: Leah Huete de Maines
Editor: Christen Kincaid
Cover Art: SunCity
Author Photo: Katherine M. Lenhart
Cover Design: Elizabeth Maines McCleavy

Order online: www.finishinglinepress.com
also available on amazon.com

Author inquiries and mail orders:
Finishing Line Press
PO Box 1626
Georgetown, Kentucky 40324
USA

Contents

I.

Against Sleepwalking	1
Yiddish	2
Mother Tongue	3
Bas Mitzvah	4
The Narrow Place—*A Midrash*	5
Howard Johnson's, Rt. 95, Jacksonville, FL	
I.	6
II.	7
III.	8
IV.	9
An Interview with the *Mogen David*	10
Why We Loved and Loathed Each Other	11
Romanian Crawl	12
Bekah on the Playground	13

II.

Origin Story	17
It Writes You	18
Sheepshead Bay, Brooklyn/Mexico City, 1968	19
Golden Rule	20
Our "Scenes of Instruction"	21
~~Whiteness: A Checklist of Excuses~~/Whiteness: What I am Making Excuses For	23
Self-Portrait with *Pentimento*	25
Death in Stratford	26
Manchester, 1972	
I. Colin	27
II. The Mother	28
III. Do-Over	29
IV. It Means	31
V. Study Abroad	32
VI. The Photo	33
Whitewashed	34

III.

Surge	39
Mother-in-Law	40
Dear *Zayde* Israel,	41
Bekah in Middle School	42
The Beginning of Understanding	43
Hall of Mirrors	44
Self-Portrait with *Kintsugi*	45
Neighborhood Bar, Pacific Heights, 1984	46
Hanover, NH, 1984-85	
I. Charisma Calling	47
II. Blindspot	48
III. *Chutzpah* in the Boardroom	49
IV. Anti-Aubade	50
Abolition Duplex	51
Prayer for the Broken	52
Hearing You	53
"The Long-Distance Runner"	54
In My Name	55
Dividing River	57
Glossary of Yiddish Words and Phrases	58
Notes	60
Acknowledgments	62

I want to be exempt [from dealing with race]. I feel, wrongly, that I should be exempt from this work because I am talking about feminism, because I am a Jew. ... These things exempt me from nothing.
 —Rachel Zucker

When it comes to race and representation, you and I are trying to make amends for the sins of our shared past while also working with still-incomplete knowledge, both about ourselves and about how we understand who, or what, constitutes "the Other."
 —Paisley Rekdal

The line snaps—
Unmoored, set loose

Into the space
Between one bank

And the other.

I.

Against Sleepwalking

It *is* easy to forget, as a Jew
I forget often our whiteness is

honorary, *tolerated* from the Latin word for
bearing, carrying, and enduring pain, claimed

by money-lenders suffered to underwrite white.
It is easy to forget that all bias squirms

in the same suburbs of the lizard brain
nasty with fear, bruised egos, swamp gas,

adrenaline. It is easy to forget
how readily I passed in a scrum of others

without the root of light
by which to bear, carry, endure

until I became what I had passed into.

Yiddish

How can I call you my mother tongue

When you did not birth me into speech?

Crouched under tables and behind cracked

Doors, sucking down murmurs like breast milk.

English spelled salvation but tasted like loss.

Ritual Hebrew cut formal and frosty.

You were *schmaltz* and brine in my mouth,

A fecund breath, ring shout, *Got tsu danken.*

But the *yentes* clucked, "*Feh*! not for you,"

Fearing the stain and cramp of shtetls and ghettos.

Kvelling over a house on "the Island," maybe

A yacht, those whitewashed rooms I shunned,

Muted, rushing back to the Lower East Side,

Its brash and hustle, its thousand clamoring accents.

Mother Tongue

faygala
elongate the a's to express pity for his parents
        derision for his softness
he might be your coveted hairdresser
        but, still, you gossip, what a *shanda*

fakakta
give the final k-t combo a strong tongue cluck
        finetuned frustrated disgust
FUBAR and SNAFU sound much too goofy
        for being beshat so thoroughly

shaygets and *shiksa*
from the Hebrew *sheqes*, meaning blemish, abomination
        pronounced with a detectable spit
often used for a romantic partner outside the faith
        we grew up thinking they meant "rotten meat"

a Shanda fur die goy
pronounce the g thickly, a tick less offensive than the above words
        for everyone not us
then *fakakt* yourself in front of them
        and know you've covered your entire people with shame

Bas Mitzvah

The boys did it on Saturdays
so I   Refused
        Refused because Saturdays
the Shabbos Bride
presided
Friday nights for the girls a pokey prelude
        Refused
because we were taught
by the Rabbi's wife
all hugs and bluster
not the taut scholar I aspired to be
        Refused because when I asked
the Rabbi who Cain and Abel married
if *not* their sisters   he pulled
my ears and scolded "You are too
curious for your own good"   Good
I fumed what is not good about
being curious
        Refused then actually to learn
to read Hebrew
so couldn't go with my friends in the class
who I urged
        Refuse   But they didn't
My parents not too upset because after all
I was a girl—

who then standing
before the Ark of the Law
Torah unveiled expected to be
by a God who played favorites
        —Refused.

The Narrow Place—a *Midrash*

Around the festive table
we dip our pinkies into muddy Passover wine
ten times for the ten plagues *Yahweh* flung
across Egypt to free the Hebrews.

dip dab dip dab
to siphon their pain from our pleasure

And I think, is this what *chosen* means—
playing favorites,
foisting blood and boils and gnats and palpable
darkness on our enemies,
slaying children, petrifying
Pharoah's heart into a brick.

And what is the point of intoning
over and over,
"We were once slaves in Egypt,"
      Mitzrayim, Hebrew for "the narrow place"

a place where we learned
how easily the Red Sea
became a bloody tsunami
ten measly drops no match for

so that all the narrow places in the world
feel familiar and we are called to remedy
and repair, to resist the narrowness—

And I feel myself pleading

    not us

        do not choose us

choose everyone

Howard Johnson's, Rt. 95, Jacksonville, FL

I.

We never talked about it—
how we waited at a rest stop and were never seated,
nothing was said, we were pressed into shadows,
the Florida sun glinting off my father's star.

Patiently, we waited, but were never seated,
my baby brother, bored, scampering in the tulips,
the Florida sun glinted off someone's star,
searing my twelve-year-old cheeks.

Amused, we watched my baby brother trespass the tulips,
while a crowd of families lined up quietly.
Something seared my twelve-year-old cheeks.
No one was discourteous.

The crowd of families lined up quietly,
not the second or third but tenth group behind us called to sit.
Though no one was discourteous,
we were pressed into shadows.

When not the second or third but tenth group was called,
nothing was said, we were pressed into shadows,
the Florida sun glinting in the shape of stars.
We never talked about it—

II.

Remember that time in Florida we weren't seated,
I ask my mother, now ninety. Wasn't a Howard Johnson's,

She says, but it was a Sunday, place packed with people
Dressed up from church. Children quiet and well-behaved.

We were noisy, in shorts and t-shirts. JayJay picked a tulip for me.
It felt like we waited for hours, I say. Groups behind us

Seated. Repeatedly. I always wore a big Jewish star, she says,
Wear it to this day. Never felt any antisemitism.

      There was a boy named Howie
In our high school class in Flatbush. It was

Senior prom, 1949, Waldorf Astoria still segregated.
So we snuck him in the back. Don't know

How we managed, she says dreamily,
But we did. And I stand up,

Walk to the kitchen sink,
Scrape the leftovers off the plates.

III.

Before
cradled in my family bubble
suckled by a boisterous Brooklyn tribalism
sunk in the merciful fog of adolescence

Then
a spring break family car trip
at a roadside restaurant passed over
eclipsed by the Florida sun
like an existential slap
       light pressed out of us
       us pressed out of them
blood-red tulips in the flower border pulsed
livid and surreal

After
bewildered awkward in my husk
how a stranger could grab your soft flesh and
twist until you fell whimpering to your knees
       I fell into a dim light
feeling the prickle of jeopardy
sensing the prominence of noses
hearing my parents' baby chick cheeps
and yet
registering
our skin's magic trick
picking locks
passing unremarked into most spaces
lining our nest with the fluff of like minds

IV.

One day I donned the star necklace
my father left me to feel him still.
"Do you even know what the *Mogen David* means?"
an old friend spat. I had to google it:
Yiddish for "shield of David," the shepherd
who slingshot giant Goliath, becoming king of Israel.

But the nazis perverted that symbol of divine favor
into a yellow badge of shame.
My friend escaped, though his people
perished in Auschwitz. Then Israel betrayed
its past, herding Palestinians into camps—
Setting the star aside, I missed the caress of dad's bling

a private david against countless Goliaths. Hugging
my half-Jewish children, I cautioned, "when they come for us,
they will come for you," gifting each one a *Mogen David*, which they
don't wear. And years ago, in my happy seaside place,
I bought a golden starfish necklace, its five arms flung wide
in joyous abandon I never take off.

An Interview with the *Mogen David*

Me? I debuted in the Dark Ages as a charm,
a rabbit's foot for fools to shake at harms.
But my two triangles laid over each other

and tugging in different directions feel like
a Medieval rack—The Kabbalists
welcomed this tension and kibitzed:

*savor the spirits of fire and air descending,
the heft of water and earth arising, male and female
contending, light and reflection, mercy and vengeance,*

white Jehovah and black Jehovah—
Oy, these contraries give me agita. I relish
the three-ness of me, six points finely balanced

like the hexagrams of the I-Ching. Could that be
a distant cousin? Still, I get it—Christians have the cross,
grisly even without the body, Islam sports a crescent moon

cradling a *normal* (5-pointed) star. Maybe the Jews,
harassed everywhere, needed a cool symbol
like me, mystical and geometrical, a bit akimbo,

sometimes self-satisfied, sometimes pissed off,
like when those bigot nazis turned me
into an obscene emblem they forced on their own

then offed them like vermin.
       My most memorable moment?
When Hal Baumgarten, preparing to storm that death trap

beach at Normandy, drew me on the back of his flak jacket
with a sharpie pen, fat target circled by the words,
Bronx, New York. When his buddy asked why,

this ordinary Jewish guy, whose surname
is German for "orchard," said, and I kid you not,
"Because then the bastards would have no difficulty spotting me."

Why We Loved and Loathed Each Other

Because you were achingly young
and your own mother, Brooklyn-born
far from her Polish *balebostes*, gallivanted,
boiling an egg every now and then,

you were dragged on dates with Edith,
your ravishing older sister, who,
years later at your mother's funeral,
forbade the rabbi to address the dead as "ever loved."

Because there was so little tenderness there
        so little joy
as you hustled post-war into womanhood
forbidden by your father to elope to teacher's college in Albany,

married at twenty to your best friend Dottie's brother
with the smoldering bedroom eyes—
Because it was before *The Feminine Mystique*
bus boycotts free love women's lib Ms.

Because you were pooh-poohed as artistic, bossy,
ambitious—not the happy housewife,
and I crowned quicksilver, an impetuous roller
coaster without brakes—

Because, years later, we were mistaken for sisters.

Romanian Crawl

Can we talk, Grandma Mary? You were never
Bubbe for me, the door slammed early on Yiddish
Zog nit keyn mol … Mir zaynen do!
sly undertow pulling us back to the ghetto—

like we gabbed those special sleep-over nights
above Dad's upholstery store, you
rolling my long hair into bouncy rag curls, the daily
Forverts draped over the gray formica kitchen table,

gripping the rim of a tall glass of hot tea and drinking
it through a sugar cube held on your tongue,
seeing the need, every summer, to send me away
to the Workmen's Circle camp, my parents leaving me

that first time, only seven, at the Bluebird city bus,
big trunk of carefully labelled clothes and Grandpa Israel's
scratchy wool blanket with the tulip pattern.
Sleeping in rows of metal cots in wooden bunks,

linking arms and belting out the camp song
*Kinder Ring, velt a naye, Set this
lousy camp on fire.* Hushed Shabbos dinners on
shtiller ovnt, endless spiels about our history—

lost on me, Yiddish spoken in our house
so we would *not* understand. But you
understood, driving up on visiting days
to swim in Sylvan Lake, your striking head

of silver waves held high above the water,
arms churning like creaky windmills—*Bubbe*
of the sweet tongue and comforting hands,
I beg you to explain how to birth the new world.

Bekah on the Playground

"Half," she wailed, "the girl asked if I was half

Jewish and half American." Seven or eight,

what did she know of identity by fracture?

But someone in this New England village knew,

trust-funders and flat-landers edging out

the old Yankees from colonial Connecticut,

who trekked north up the long tidal river, edging out

the Abenaki people, overrunning *Gdakinna*.

New Hampshire granite, marble of Vermont,

distinct bedrocks ground together by slow glacial pressure—

The ground churned beneath her and we,

knowing children parrot what they hear at home,

attended the principal's "listening" hours,

were assured "there was no antisemitism here, no no no,"

he said, voice keen with affront. "And, no, we don't need

to raise this with the kids, just look at the Menorah

we erect in the play yard every Christmas" (lighting the candles

from the wrong end, I screamed silently), the other parents

nodding like bobblehead dolls. My partner beamed me

a warning and gazing off, I gut-felt the rift and heave

that forged then flooded the dividing river.

II.

Origin Story

"white is not a given"
it's a taken

space
taken up in talk   in tears

work
in taking all the credit

us taken as unmarked
(all the unnoted ~~white~~ people in these poems)

take (v.)
from the Old Norse *taka* to seize

with Viking vehemence
The Oxford English Dictionary calls it

"one of the elemental words of the language"
take alone has 55 shades of meaning

as in, are we so *taken up* with eyes (ayes, I's)
so *mistaken* in that trick of veneer

or *caretaken* so *breathtaking*
can we survive without a *give-and-take*

as in *takeover   takeout   takeoff   partaker*
taken bad   painstaking   overtaken   undertaking

It Writes You

My particular whiteness, its tumults and evasions.

Invisible gas I acclimate to breathing.

Spoiling my pages with cross-outs and ink blots.

There it is: my self expressed as a neutral white background

Blotted by errant black marks.

But isn't mold white?

Is it even possible to see the ground

When I am lifted almost without effort?

Sheepshead Bay, Brooklyn/Mexico City, 1968

And my parents clucking at the TV
spewed the familiar Yiddish slur
for the two US runners on the medal podium, heads bowed,
gloved hands raised in the Black power salute.

My teenage eyes snapped into focus—
the loud floral drapes and matching slipcovers
dad sewed in his shop on Coney Island Avenue
for the pull-out living room couch he slept on with mom,
the caged parakeet, one of many, who ate from their hands,
a few books but many *Look* and *Life* magazines,
stereo dishing out Sinatra, Tony Bennett, Johnny Mathis and,
of course, the divine Barbra—

"It's the fault of the system," I flung back like a slap,
        parroting my recent reading of Brown's
        Manchild in the Promised Land.

They gaped at me, their daughter suddenly
a stranger babbling nonsense about passing—

Mom heaved up to refill her seltzer. Dad
reached over to change the channel.

Golden Rule

I write, scrambling through a bramble of slurs,
slung at my people and the people we put down,

defiled, then defiling others in all the barbed wire
places peddling myths about what makes us free.

The groups we demean, are they our buffer
against rock-bottom or do we fear having to share

scraps of capitalism's poisoned pie, scrabbling
to stand on bent backs to catch a sliver of sky?

How to unlearn this toxic alphabet, sludge
in unwitting mouths that kissed me

goodnight as a child, lessons I assimilated asleep,
waking to my own bleached tongue, mouth sliced

by switchblade sticks, stones piled like pyramids—
How not to do to others what was done to us.

Our "Scenes of Instruction"

I.

Cruising in the snazzy baby blue El Dorado, windows down, tape deck blasting Olivia Newton-John. Off I95, a few blocks into gritty Baltimore, my mother says, "put up your window, this is the bad part of town." Another day, same car, same mother, older me. Stopped at a light downtown, a man in the next car very close smiles. I smile back. My mother says, "never smile at Black men, it's dangerous."

Gone already twenty years—how long will this message survive her?

II.

I grew up in Roanoke, Louisiana, a village bisected by railroad tracks. On one side, the Black part of town called "The Quarters," a name I didn't question then. One day, at the Post Office, a little Black boy my age said, "Hello, S—." We were both about five years old. This was 1956 or 57. His mother yanked him hard by the hand and dragged him out, pure terror contorting her face.

Looking around for what had frightened her, I saw all the big people calmly waiting in line to buy stamps and mail packages, no clue to the madness white girls could unleash.

III.

In my college astronomy class, we learned that at the center of our universe is a massive—no, the prof said, "supermassive black hole" named Sagittarius A*, 4.2 million times as large as our sun. Though it's 25,800 light years away, it exerts an enormous gravitational pull on the orbits of planets and, also, my textbook warned, threatens to draw everything into its immense lightless void. I imagined our Milky Way, a brilliant white arc pebbling the sky like thick cream poured into black coffee not yet stirred, sucked up by a giant angry black vacuum cleaner. I wondered why 'Sagittarius' and learned from *Wikipedia* that it is an astrological sign associated with the archer Chiron, who is a centaur, half human and half horse, famous for his wisdom and knowledge of healing.

Why describe the heart of our universe as an angry *black* superforce of cosmic annihilation and name it for a figure outside the human, adjacent to the bestial, bridled, ridden on, and reined in?

IV.

Strolling through New Haven, my beloved adopted home dappled like sunlight and shadow through willows, where no group has sway. I catch sight of my pale bare arms and feel them to be—uncanny, a thing separate from me like a sleeve of meat, marbled white.

~~Whiteness: A Check List of Excuses~~
Whiteness: What I am Making Excuses For

~~Have been unaware of my privileges as white.~~
Have been lifted up without sensing or caring who is put down.

~~Really unaware of my privileges as a white woman.~~
How doors are held opened, if condescendingly,
and my pain is unquestioningly acknowledged.

~~Protested that I know and like many people of color.~~
That I know and like some people of color but always feel a gap, a gripe, the old agenda.

~~That I have Black friends.~~
Not nearly enough friends not nearly enough closeness.

~~That I had a Black boyfriend.~~
That I fell into liking him despite myself.

~~That I had *two* Black boyfriends.~~
That something so shockingly deep in me responded to him, and yet—

~~That I am a good person~~
That goodness is not even skin-deep.

~~Who marched during the 60s.~~
Who marched and protested but slunk back to my comfort zone.

~~Cried when friends pointed out my racist language.~~
Cried, ashamed, appalled without really comprehending the depth of the hurt.

~~Feared when I passed a dark man on a dark street.~~
Feared darkness as a rut in the brain I struggled to dig out of.

~~Did not call out racism when I saw it.~~
Failed so many times, continue to fail to call out racism.

~~Retreated into my tribe to complain about "the complainers."~~
Surrendered to the downy nest of my tribe.

~~Felt exhausted by the awareness of racism and wanted it to go away.~~
Can we all just get along???

~~Consumed Black culture and felt cool about it.~~
Did not, could not interrogate the blues at the root of my soul as appropriation.

~~Got frustrated by the shifting terminology around race and color.~~
Kicked myself for my lack of patience, my patronizing—but not hard.

~~Felt checked, cornered, rejected like a bounced check.~~
Felt the discomfort of being unchecked, the freedom of not having to know.

~~Just wanted it to go away.~~
Just want it to go a different way—for everyone.

Self-Portrait with *Pentimento*

In the novel, Lucrezia de' Medici
Ached to paint herself
With a brush of mouse hair
Tiny scenes of transgression   All she was
Not allowed to do or be
Then whitewashed them   and painted over
Willows   a moat   the dowry of sky—
Repenting nothing

In his elegy for his son
Ed Hirsch called upon the God
Of Scribbles and Erasures   to fix
The mercurial boy   but failing
Imagined himself Giacometti
Scraping the canvas bare
Over and over   Hugging air
Repenting all

I weigh these approaches
To my own likeness—
Fog, skunk, and con games—
Camouflaging or scraping down
The repentant self
Like trying to stroke the tigress
Caged in the Duke's cellars
Keening for its wild

Death in Stratford

At the bridge across the placid Avon
we meet Othello and Desdemona
on bikes only moments after the matinee performance
smiling, full of breath.
They seem like an item.

My gut still clenched
throat choked

       I'd forgotten that
driven into a jealous rage by evil Iago,
Othello kills Desdemona
twice,
first smothered while swearing he will love her
"after,"
then, like a candle refusing to be snuffed,
strangled with her own sheets,
forgiveness staining her lips.

"How do you act it over and over?" I croak.
Swans litter the river path with feathers and
tang the August air with guano.

"The audience," she says. "That you get it.
That they are both victims of white patriarchy
but resist it
by loving, dying, Othello killing her and then himself out of a world
they cannot survive in—"

When I vow *never to watch the play again
where loving to death is the only resistance,*
they turn their backs,
mount their seats and
ride off—together.

Manchester, 1972

I. Colin

I'm centrifugal and love the color
burgundy, loved it before it became
the new black. I've never met a rule I don't want
to break. Breakage was the rule back then
when black had only just become
beautiful—for some of us. Remember?
In the gray-toned photo, now
a half-century old, you are
beautiful. You suffuse the center,
your high, pointed Afro prominent
against bare Lowland trees. Lips parted,
you must be speaking with that West Indian lilt
tinged with Cockney thrilling to my raw American ears. We were
twenty, and I was far from home. I became beautiful
when Barbra Streisand shocked Johnny Carson's late-night show
jangling a ring of keys and purring *any place I hang my hat.*
In the photo I stand
at the edge in beaded bell bottoms
and a burgundy evening jacket lined with seal.
My whole being yearns towards you. Did we
share a bed? I cannot remember
your last name. The photo shows distant
buildings stark and dumb.
Not your long slender hands always in motion
like a maestro or magician.
Your swagger and banter
in the rain-slicked freezing mud.

II. Your Mother

She was large, forbidding, commanding
the tiny kitchen of the dim flat
in Brixton, I think it was.
My kid sister Michelle visiting from the States,

we hitchhiked there from Manchester.
Did she cook for us? Where did we
sleep? I remember your mother fussing over
Mich, it was me she resented,

sucking her teeth, clicking her tongue.
When I asked why, oblivious,
you replied, as if it were obvious,
"she hates that I have

a white girlfriend." I stopped
you, then, with a fierce kiss,
the lions of Trafalgar Square cryptic
in the endless drizzle.

III. Do-Over

You, Colin's mother, are probably long gone.

I am stranded in the third decade
of the 21st century, "post-racial" by some accounts,

confronted by my failure of interest in
Who You Were.

When your only son arrived at your Brixton flat
with a hippy white girl, American no less, you

sucked your teeth, gave me the stink eye.
A lumbering obstacle to my 1970's study abroad

Jouissance. Can we have a do-over?
Meet at some Soho pop-up and sift through

racks searching for the perfect useless (what you all call) *frock*.
Or stroll into the Shoreditch "Facebar" redolent with

aspiration, where you could achieve the best you and
I could achieve the best me, perceiving each other

through the grift of newness, sipping mineral water laced with lime.
Who would serve us? Edgy artists of the articulate brow

or immigrants from yet another wave, doing mani-pedis,
blurry photos of distant loved ones tacked on the walls.

Would you be willing to forgive
my obtuseness? Could we untangle the scripts

we played into and out. Is it naive to think I could
select a rich shade of coral lipstick to complement

your skin tone and it would mean only that.
And you could steer me away from the black leather miniskirt

with zippers askew and it would mean only that.
And we could embrace the striving artists and immigrants,

and our prior and present made-up selves.

IV. It Means

Mashed tatties crowned with a layer of heavy cream
browned under the broiler, when sliced into with a fork
oozed out rich white lava. Taste unforgettable
though I cannot remember your last name.
Back then this felt decadent and delicious, but now
it means you cooked for me in the pokey back kitchen
of the Levenshulme flat I rented with Sally and Fran,
two English girls I met at university.
Means we cooked and ate together,
were not just a randy study abroad hook-up,
counter culture's *love-the-one-you're-with* thing.

Your supple hands washing up in the sink's pink plastic tub,
you didn't rinse the soap off the dishes,
saving the 10 p coins we used to feed the water heater
next to the WC. Strange to an American but
it means your feisty mama
trained you well in domestic arts, in economy,
didn't feel her boy was above shopping,
cooking for himself, washing up,
being independent, making your way
in a world where
skin color meant something I couldn't fathom.

V. Study Abroad

Mashed tatties crowned with heavy cream, browned under the broiler—

> Butcher's knives, iron bars, and Teddy Boys muscling into West Indian neighborhoods—

You cooking in the pokey kitchen of the Levenshulme flat I shared with Sally and Fran—

> Oswald Mosely, founder of the British Union of Fascists, braying "Keep Britain White"—

Washing dishes in the sink's pink plastic tub, laughing easily, sharing chores—

> Guyana finally cutting the strings tying it to Britain in 1966—

Always in motion, you rocked a camel-hair overcoat from the high street's charity shop—

> Notting Hill Carnival gets lively-upped every August, drawing millions—

Singed cream oozing, scalding milky tea and touches, your charring lips—

> Tang of jerk chicken and curried goat, soca and reggae blasting from every speaker—

Your Guyanese mama stink-eyed my white ass but raised you well—

> Everyone grooving and mingling together in the soggy London heat—

Your skin a secret memo tangled up in my budding awareness—

> "Windrush" West Indians brought over post-war to rebuild Britain, deported in 2018—

VI. The Photo

taken as the gaggle of university friends tumbled out and posed in a line against the van. In memory it glows red and merry like the Merry Pranksters, but we jolted along rutted back roads in the frozen mud and Scotland's horizontal winter rain. Shivering. Loads of herbal refreshment. We were celebrating winter birthdays—those who achieved twenty. In the background, buildings loom farm-industrial with only a fringe of bare trees against a blank sky. On the left, two Americans. Judy, open like a spring day. A tiny girl whose huge breasts got badly singed by the sun camping in a cave above Mylopotas on Ios over our spring break. And Deb, head tilted slyly, which she was. We hitched across England harmonizing on "Norwegian Wood" and "Yesterday" for randy truckers. Maxine from Germany laughing, snugged up to Finn, a lanky handsome Dane in a fisherman's sweater and slouch hat. Sally, from Birmingham, glamorous in a full-length fox coat, delicate granny glasses on her fine-boned face, pale skin set off by raven hair, head thrown back flirtatiously. A Carnaby Street siren. Behind her, you occupy the center. The only one turned away, your Afro high and pointed against the barren trees. I stand off to the right with Anne. In beaded bell bottoms and an evening jacket lined in seal. Though we talk, I furtively look past Anne, cutting my eyes away from her friendly homely face, my smile forced, trying to focus on her words, to be in the now of the then, not in the urgent pull of your orbit.

Whitewashed

> "White is transcendent and timeless, with unrivaled versatility."
> —Benjamin Moore

Light sheering off white stone.

White walls and ceilings, billowing white curtains.

Bleached trees. Bleached grass. Bleached flowers.

Even the sun a pallid glare.

Icy wind breathed in like splintered mirrors.

Sanitized. Absolved. At least, that's how it often feels.

*

Everything uncolored, arranged, deranged, obstructively transparent—

white lies
whited sepulcher
white man's burden
white noise
White River Junction
men in white coats
White House
white out
white knights
Great White Hope
white flight
white guilt
carte blanche
as the driven snow

*

Surreptitiously, I unsheathe a tiny shiv
smuggled in under my tongue—the blade
dwarfed by the misty immensity of the abyss,
and begin chipping.

I sense others around me, restive, ghostly, hooded.
Some furtive, some bold, many flailing, weak
from lack of substance. Faded Ahabs.

Others clamor behind invisible walls.

Ground littered with policy papers, the shriveled
carcasses of charitable donations.

I chip, scrape, sliver …

Trifling flakes sink into the void, so little has changed.

CHIP …

My pocked knife could be your crooked crowbar, your gilded shovel.

I pare off layers of nacreous pearl

searching for the core, the provoking grain,

the scarred and tender unwritten flesh.

III.

Surge

when my belly filled
then emptied

my breasts filled
then emptied

daily for months
they surfaced—

the silvery stretch marks
I tried to swab away with cocoa butter

hieroglyphs of the body
breaching its skin

as the self, cresting, labors
to crack itself open

to a world
bound by someone else's
bargains of power

bellied white sails
threading
rough shallows

as waters rush
to flood
the wide river delta—

now I pry myself open
and submit to the swell

a wreck tumbling in surf
emptying then filling

Mother-in-Law

That doozie day you saw me
After months of eye-slide and glare,
And though I was part of the family
You were bound to the Lord,

A lord with foreign features
Who cut a razor line
'Tween saints and sinners, false and true,
And I was none of good.

A stranger like a storm cloud
Brought tempests to your cup,
By not embracing your world view
And caused you a mortal hurt.

I endured the scrutiny,
Answering curt with grace
Until you said, "I like your rings,"
And named me with your smile.

An intimate world fell open,
One so rarely found,
Where something tiny like a like
Can strike away the blind.

Dear *Zayde* Israel,

This is your granddaughter, Ivy, Harold's oldest.
I often sense you close, though we never met,
bear the burden as your namesake, "Israel,"
meaning "one who struggles with God,"
the name bestowed on Jacob after wrestling
the Angel, and adopted by the cocky
Jewish nation. How there, do I, a woman,
Carry your name and claim my own place?

I reach for the fire that drove you
on Sundays into Tompkins Square Park
haranguing your socialist gospel: power
in the people, in work, above all, in the collective,
daring me to embody your spirit, scorched tongue,
scorched face, mute and blinded in my own way.

Bekah in Middle School

Beating small fists on her burning face
hunched on a chair pulled up
to my desk in the laundry room
awash in student essays, bookshelves
wedged between washer and dryer.

On the playground big boys
called a smaller boy "gay."
Puzzling it over on the school bus home,
she thought of our friends Lisa and Lexi,
the wedding of Sam and Quinn in the Thetford church,
their long, long kiss.

"What would Rosie the Riveter do?" I asked,
one of her namesakes. Silence.
Essays rustled restlessly for grades.
"Maybe write a letter to the principal?" I tried.
    "Can a good girl
do that?" she squeaked.
Alarms clanged in my head,
the words *good* and *girl* tangoing across a minefield.

"Remember our promise in Karate,
at the beginning of each class,
to defend the path of truth."
So we sounded out
        "homophobia"
and she conjured the playground
a green space grown over with grass and clover.
"I hope … I hope … I hope …" she scrawled
on the big yellow legal pad in her best looping script.

Next day she came home aghast
her letter read out in every homeroom,
so we hugged and high-fived
but kept the imaginary sleeves of Rosie's blue work shirt
rolled up.

The Beginning of Understanding
for Michael Brown

When your neighbor cried on the news
*four and a half hours he lay
in the hot street just down from my door*
and the interviewer repeated
      hours

suddenly the word
broke inside me
swelled, pressing against
the inside of my skull
my pale hands, suddenly
surprised by the fact
of the knife, clutched
the half-sliced lemon
on the cutting board
near the tall glass of ice water
as the clock above the counter
droned on

Hall of Mirrors

All I see is a shapely red dress
hanging like emptied fruit.
How slender the blossomed body that filled it,
I think, when my companion points to a sign
and whispers, "What is #*MMIW*?" as we
blunder into a thicket of hanging red dresses
each releasing the distinct musk of its wearer.

Over 5700 Missing and Murdered
Indigenous Women and Girls

wrenched from reservations
where blurry laws jimmy loopholes
for slime to crawl through.

Then I remember myself—
white woman of an age, knee jerk reaction
seeing the crimson of passion and rebellion
in shapes of beauty I envied.

Not what red means in many Native cultures—
the only color spirits perceive,
hung up by the living
to beckon back
the souls
of the disappeared.

Self-Portrait with *Kintsugi*

a shapely porcelain bowl
safe on a high shelf
above everyday use
holding   precisely nothing
shaken free by a quake or quirk
or the beat of clamoring feet
tips from its privileged perch
to meet the unforgiving ground

dried marigolds and red dust
from unmarked graves
steeped in muddy river water
and tears
then molded into an earthy
gold to fill the cracks

Neighborhood Bar, Pacific Heights, 1984

It started casually over Chivas and a splash,
pondering Jesse Jackson's Rainbow Coalition
with a close friend, fiercest spirit I knew.
When her magical man succumbed to cancer after 'Nam,
I dared her to go to law school. She emerged
relentless.

We wondered, should we uplift what we all share
or how we differ? She passionately championed
our commonalities.
This struck me as
color blind to the history of hurts and wrongs,
boiling us down to a common white male denominator.

It got heated.

Suddenly, we were screaming,
digging into our positions faster than the Viet Cong.
Heads turned. Time stopped.
The sacred spring of friendship poisoned
by either/or.

Hanover, NH, 1985/86
for G.R.

I. Charisma Calling

Hunger in his voice,
part preacher, part partisan

he works the rainbow crowd
swelling Shabbaz Hall,

breathing a single aspiration:
imagining the world otherwise

together. "We must
be the change we seek,"

he chants and beckons me
forward. Under

pressure, words that I
do not know I know, spill

from a shell he's cracked.
They are acceptable

to the cause. Later,
in the dark, his charisma

charge, electric kiss, we
sizzle until

he's gone, answering another
urgent call.

II. Blindspot

Did I think I could
leave white behind?
Purge my flesh
in his force field
or have him
rearrange my
cellular charge?

Did I think his smolder
would break me open
or cleanse me of my history,
my Jewishness suddenly
a portal and not a wall?

I yearned
to be
drawn
like a thorn
out of the
poisoned
eye

III. *Chutzpah* in the Boardroom

Three white men, college trustees, commanding the space, at ease.
As if by birthright, they occupy the elegant hall
now eerily empty of students. Hearing the verdict—
the shanty-smashers would go free—
a dozen die-hard divestment protesters
armed with sleeping bags and Franz Fanon
marched up to the bell tower in the library's summit
modelled on Philadelphia's Independence Hall.

When the board arrives in town, the tower's light blazes green—
for money? Or the Great Gatsby's grasping for
"the orgiastic future that year by year
                                      recedes before us."

Deputed by the protestors as go-betweens, you and I
pulled these three pillar men from an elegant dinner,
begging them *not* to order the occupiers,
who were the age of their children,
strapped into sleds and lowered down the face of the tower. Two
hundred feet. In the dark.

It was your body language that slayed me.
Eye to eye, shoulder to shoulder with the men
your Blackness didn't matter.
Your tone deliberate, persuasive,
companionable gruff chuckle edged with the slightest
sliver of mock.
I sensed some familiar fume suffusing
the stately hall, ruffling the velvet curtains,
a heady dialect of cigar smoke, snipped tips, and brandy.
On the edge, I writhed,
a frenzy, riot, hot wire about to short.
Could have stripped and spit nickels
on the glossy black and white parquet floor without
breaking your stride.

IV. Anti-Aubade

Couldn't refuse (you anything) when you asked to borrow my car.

Boston, you said, just for the day, not far.

Driving while Black with a tiny vial up the interstate.

That night, euphoria slammed us like lifers without parole miraculously reprieved.

Was there ever any time except this now   here   fused?

How to write an elegy for ecstasy.

Soul mates though intellectually I reject that concept.

How you kept yourself regally closed and I (thought I) offered everything.

Your heart-breaking need to be fathomless and sunk in sensation.

To escape the frenzy of invisible dogs you seemed to sense at your heels.

Lover, I cooed, *let's save some for tomorrow.*

You sprinting up and down the stairs to that vial in the car until there was nothing left.

Abolition Duplex
      after Jericho Brown

What prayer might persuade police
To throw off the yoke of choke holds?

      Can *serve and protect* ever be expressed by a choke hold?
      Can a choke hold ever reclaim a breath?

What breath is reclaimed as they ram knees to throat?
What can't they grasp in the words, *I can't breathe*?

      If we cannot breathe, we cannot speak or sing, exchanging
      essence, me and you, us and them trading molecules of air

So close the molecules bear an offering of ourselves.
All the selves on offer as we walk our neighborhood.

      Police walk neighborhoods they don't live in, love in,
      Don riot gear, face shields, wield mace pepper spray.

Emily Dickinson put mace in her famous "black cake."
What prayer might persuade?

Prayer for the Broken

I pray
though my faith in *Yahweh*, in any god
who can hear is severely shattered

I pray
most often to a goddess of settling,
Shekhinah, shy volatile spirit of spirit

I pray
when in motion:
loping through neighborhoods

weeding
and deadheading
not solely in my own plot

I pray
in accents foreign to my own ears
after talking to my suffering loved ones

I pry
my lips between desire and reprieve,
tonguing phrases that often slip away

I play
endless games in my
head with my head

*Al molay rachamim, shochayn bam'romim,
ham-tzay m'nucha n'chona al kanfay Hash'china*

I pray
that I learn to greet
others and recreate what whole is

Hearing You
    for June Jordan

At first I thought you were angry
at having been plucked from the plush solitude
of the writer's retreat.
But in the car you shared how much
you missed your city kitchen, your people
how you would stay in Peterborough just until the poems
ran out, how in that tight space
you needed to focus before giving your keynote address and turned
slightly from me
closed your eyes and—withdrew.

And I chafed at the stilled brown sliver of your face
refusing to give me back myself.
I did not see then it was
my raw white feminist longing
you had to escape,
expecting an easy sisterhood,
needing assurance that I was part of the solution,
or how I wanted to be borne
on a back already burdened
by being thought to be
 "wrong," to be "the history of
     rape,"

and by my need to be taught
and specifically by you

even there
in the silence of that car.

"The Long-Distance Runner"
for Grace Paley

O still unchecked luminary at our seders, readings, prison performances, weekly Protest of Women in Black against the Occupation who, in the early 2000s, stood presciently on the corner of Wheelock and Main. When I got up the nerve to ask you to visit my class, we talked about your story's protagonist and your persona, Jewish and middle-aged Faith, who suddenly took up running, ran back to her old Brooklyn neighborhood turned mostly Black, and lived for three surreal weeks in her old apartment now occupied by Mrs. Luddy, her four kids, stinky diapers, and welfare checks.

My questions were endless.

"Faith runs away from her comfy Manhattan home, returns to her Jewish immigrant origins, and becomes like a child again, right? Essentially enters the life of a single Black mother on welfare, experiences its stark differences from her own? Faith wants to be intimate like sisters, share confidences and yearnings, but Mrs. Luddy's a realist and deflects her overtures? Our worlds, seemingly so distant and foreign, doom us to separation, mistrust, misunderstanding? White women are so naive about race and white privilege they literally have to be forced to smell the shit? We are supposed to learn from Faith's mistakes, her unconscious biases, her blindness to a structural analysis? And what's with all the curse words, racial slurs, writing in Black urban voices in this story?"

Ivy, you drawled, *don't analyze so much.*

In My Name

plush on tongues that first called me
my name's Yiddish endearment:
      Ívelah

sometimes even more intimate
just "I"
low and long in the mouth
"I" called to fish sticks and creamed corn
"I" called to have her headstrong hair brushed

so frequent
whenever grade school teachers uttered the word "I"
I snapped to attention

clung to that odd plant name
through sneering serenades of the late fifties hit, "Poison Ivy"
      you're gonna need an ocean (bop doo wop)
      of calamine lotion

bristled hearing it on another,
seeing it signed on paper money by the second woman US treasurer

names answering a sacramental call
necessary for exorcism or blessing

grown years later
meeting a person of the same name who presented
Black and male and not green at all
who hailed me mouthing *our* name—wryly,
gingerly, like twins
      separated at birth
like he'd already spied me bare-assed,
fate or mothers having plucked the same
image of vine and twining
for this   male   outwardly so *not*   me

my singularity cracked   in half
broke me open

but he inhabited us so well
I felt my "I" doubling
like dough kneaded, punched down and finally proofed.

Dividing River

Of course, there are no trails. No maps
or instructions. The grass thigh high,

tips pearled with dew flung off
by my hiking boots. I follow the reek

of mud and something more—elemental.
At the edge, water churns to a frenzy

by unseasonable rains, daisies and black-
eyed susans tap deep into the muck,

their black and white and gold
beckon me through the mystic day

until, on the far side, a bridge unfurls
near willows flecked by sun and shadow—

Here yes here is the place to cross over

Glossary of Yiddish words and phrases

See also: https://mameloshn.org/2019/11/19/the-yiddish-handbook-40-words-you-should-know/

Balebostes	A good homemaker, and a woman thoroughly in charge of her home.
Bas Mitzvah	Literally, "daughter of commandment." When a Jewish girl turns 12, she undergoes a public ceremony of initiation into all the rights and obligations of a Jewish adult, including the commandments of the Torah, becoming part of the Jewish community. The male equivalent is Bar Mitzvah, literally, "son of commandment."
Bubbe	Grandmother.
Chutzpah	Audacity, for good or bad; an English equivalent is "hubris." From a Hebrew word meaning "insolence" or "cheek."
Feh!	An expression of disgust or disapproval, representing the sound of spitting and sometimes accompanied by vigorous finger shaking.
Forverts	Literally, "Forward," the name of a Yiddish-language daily newspaper launched in 1897. Under the leadership of its founding editor, Abraham Cahan, it came to be known as the voice of the Jewish immigrant, fighting for social justice, democracy and Jewish rights. https://forward.com/about-us/history/
Got tsu danken	Thank God.
Kinder Ring, velt a naye	"The children's circle, a new world." It is the first line of the alma mater of Camp Kinder Ring, located on Sylvan Lake in the Peekskill Mountains of New York. It was founded in 1927 by the Workmen's

	(now Workers) Circle, a Jewish socialist organization, to give its members and their children a place for summer vacations and immersion in Yiddish culture.
Kvelling	To swell with pride at the achievements of loved ones.
Schmaltz	Rendered chicken or goose fat, an integral ingredient in traditional Ashkenazi Jewish cuisine, used as a cooking fat, spread, or flavoring.
Shtiller ovnt	Literally, "quiet evening," denoting the contemplative atmosphere of Friday nights and the celebration of Shabbos, the beginning of the Jewish day of rest. See https://www.campkr.com/friday-evenings/
Yentes	Female gossips or busy-bodies.
Zayde	Grandfather.

Zog nit keyn mol … Mir zaynen do!
"Never say … We are here!" Part of the first line (used as a title) and the refrain of the "Partisan Song" composed by Hersh Glick, a Jewish resistance fighter in the Vilna Ghetto of what is now Lithuania, who was killed in 1944 at the age of 24. The song became a rallying cry for Jews in the darkest days of the Holocaust and is a symbol of resistance.

Notes

Zucker epigraph is from "Exempt, Implicated" in *The Racial Imaginary: Writers on Race in the Life of the Mind*, edited by Claudia Rankine, Beth Loffreda, Max King Cap, 2014, p. 175.

Rekdal epigraph is from A*ppropriate: A Provocation*, 2021, p. 11.

"Against Sleepwalking" responds to Whoopi Goldberg's comments on "The View," on January 31, 2021, that the Holocaust was "not about race" for which she was publicly upbraided and suspended from the show for two weeks.

"Sheepshead Bay/Mexico City 1968." *Manchild in the Promised Land* (1965) is the popular autobiography by Claude Brown, about growing up in Harlem, NY during the 1940s and 1950s.

"Romanian Crawl." The Workmen's (now Workers) Circle was founded in 1900 by progressive Jewish immigrants to the US to advance social justice and Jewish culture.

"Our 'Scenes of Instruction'" was inspired by Ailish Hopper's essay, "The Gentle Art of Making Enemies" in the collection *A Sense of Regard: Essays on Poetry and Race*, edited by Laura McCullough, 2015, 183-198. "Scenes of Instruction" is Henry Louis Gates's term for the traumatic moments, often violent, in which Black people are made to feel their racialization as inferiority.

"Origin Story." The opening line is from Martha Collins, *Blue Front: A Poem*. The source for information on "take" is from "etymology online" at https://www.etymonline.com/word/take

"Self-Portrait with *Pentimento*." The first stanza draws on Maggie O'Farrell's historical novel, *The Marriage Portrait* (2022). The second stanza draws on Ed Hirsch's book-length poem *Gabriel* (2014).

"Dear *Zayde* Israel." Among Ashkenazi Jews, it is traditional to name children after relatives who have died as a way to keep their memory alive and to inspire the namesake to live up to their predecessor's better qualities. The child is often given a name with the same first letter as their namesake's name.

"Self-Portrait with *Kintsugi*." Kintsugi, Japanese for "golden joinery," is the art of repairing broken pottery by filling the cracks with an adhesive dusted with powdered gold or silver. The philosophy is that breakage and repair are part of the history of the object, not to be disguised but integral to its beauty of brokenness.

"Prayer for the Broken." The Hebrew translates as "God, full of mercy, Who dwells above, give rest on the wings of the Divine Presence [*Shekhinah*]," considered a feminine principle.

"Hearing You." The quotations are from June Jordan's incomparable "Poem about my Rights."

"In My Name." The second woman to become US Treasurer was Ivy Baker Priest, from 1953-1961.

Acknowledgments

Thanks to the following publications, in which these poems first appeared, sometimes in different form or with different titles:

Bloodroot Literary Magazine: "'Four and a Half'" [now "The Beginning of Understanding"], "System Within" [now "Hall of Mirrors"], "Death in Stratford"

Feminists Talk Whiteness, edited by Janet Gray: "White Me: A Checklist" [now "Whiteness: A Checklist of Excuses/Whiteness: What I am Making Excuses For"], which also appeared in *Within Flesh: In Conversation with Our Selves and Emily Dickinson*, by Al Salehi and Ivy Schweitzer, Transcendent Zero Press, 2024 as "Redeemable Checkpoints"

Mid-Atlantic Review, special section on "The Jewish Experience:" "Bas Mitzvah"

Mississippi Review, "Whitewashed"

New Croton Review, "Bekah in Middle School," "Impossible" [now "As If"], "That Means [now "It Means]," "Bekah on the Playground," "Starfish" [now "Howard Johnson's, off Rt. 95, Jacksonville, FL IV]

New England Poetry Club, "Manchester," selected by Enzo Silon Surin as Honorable Mention for the Samuel Allen Washington Prize for a long poem or sequence.

Passager, Poetry Contest: "Howard Johnson's, off Rt. 95, Jacksonville, FL I"

Ritualwell, "Prayer for the Broken"

Spoon River Poetry Review, "Pentimento" [now "Self-Portrait with Pentimento"] and "Do-Over"

Tikkun, "Against Sleepwalking"

Within Flesh: In Conversation with Our Selves and Emily Dickinson, by Al Salehi and Ivy Schweitzer, Transcendent Zero Press, 2024: "Refreshing Color" [now "It Writes You"]; "Officers of the Peace" [now "Abolition Duplex"], "Breathtaking Justice" [now "The Beginning of Understanding"]

Deepest gratitude to Charif Shanahan, who brought this project to life and remains its guiding spirit. And to Vievee Francis, whose generosity, patience and fierceness are a model for me. Sincere thanks to Lynn Melnick for hearing and helping to dis/order the poems, Catherine Barnett for generous suggestions, Jan Freeman for the gift of details and the wonderful "poetry games." To Rich Michelson for being a mensch and Heid Erdrich for her friendship and presence. Big thanks to my poetry buddies: Lisa Furmanski, who patiently read this manuscript in its many versions; Giavanna Munafo, who read it over with a generous and expert eye; Ewa Chrusciel, Marisa Miller Donovan, Nancy Crumbine, Jane Ackerman. To Thomas Luxon, for valuable feedback and endless support, and Ellen Miller-Mack, whose unerring eye for the squishy parts helped make the poems stronger. And to Joan Houlihan and Carey Salerno at the Colrain Manuscript Review Conference, who gave support at a crucial time.

Ivy Schweitzer is the co-author of two poetry collections with Al Salehi, an Iranian-American poet based in California. *Within Flesh: In Conversation with Our Selves and Emily Dickinson*, appeared from Transcendent Zero Press in February 2024. They have completed a second collection, *Broken Open: Practicing Humanity with Rumi*, about the conflict in Gaza. *Dividing Rivers* is her debut solo collection.

Her poetry has appeared, most recently, in *Passager, Ritualwell, Tikkun, New Croton Review, Mississippi Review, Spoon River Poetry Review, Mid-Atlantic Review,* The New England Poetry Club's Prize *Winners' Anthology 2024* and *The Mountain Troubadour* from the Poetry Society of Vermont. She has read, most recently, at the Howe Library, Left Banks Books and Still North Books in Hanover, NH, and at the Hartland, VT Poetry Festival.

Born in Brooklyn, NY, Ivy Schweitzer has lived for many years in Vermont and taught English and Women's, Gender, and Sexuality Studies at Dartmouth College. She is the creator of White Heat: Dickinson in 1862, a weekly blog and collaborated on *HomeWorks,* a digital pedagogical site that offers lessons from 19th women writers about the richness of staying at home. She serves on the Board and as the Website Director of the Emily Dickinson International Society. For more on her poetry and professional work, visit her author page at https://sites.dartmouth.edu/ivyschweitzer/

www.ingramcontent.com/pod-product-compliance
Lightning Source LLC
Chambersburg PA
CBHW030057170426
43197CB00010B/1563